POLAND

A Troubled Past, A New Start

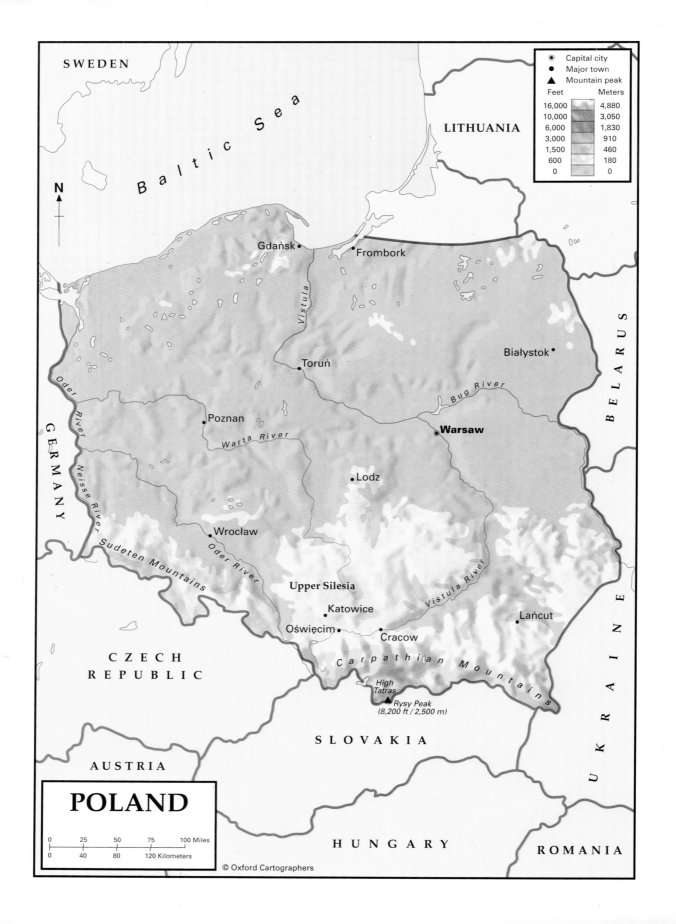

SWEDEN

Baltic Sea

LITHUANIA

BELARUS

N

Gdańsk ●

● Frombork

Vistula

Toruń ●

Białystok ●

Bug River

GERMANY

Oder River

Neisse River

Poznan ●

Warta River

Warsaw ⊙

Lodz ●

Wrocław ●

Oder River

Sudeten Mountains

Vistula River

Upper Silesia

Katowice ●

Lańcut ●

Oświęcim ●

● Cracow

CZECH REPUBLIC

Carpathian Mountains

High Tatras

▲ *Rysy Peak*
(8,200 ft / 2,500 m)

UKRAINE

SLOVAKIA

AUSTRIA

HUNGARY

ROMANIA

POLAND

0 25 50 75 100 Miles
0 40 80 120 Kilometers

© Oxford Cartographers

EXPLORING CULTURES OF THE WORLD

POLAND

A Troubled Past, A New Start

Eleanor H. Ayer

MARSHALL CAVENDISH

NEW YORK

*W*ith thanks to Dr. Thaddeus V. Gromada of the
Polish Institute of Arts and Sciences, New York City,
for his expert reading of the manuscript.

Benchmark Books
Marshall Cavendish Corporation
99 White Plains Road
Tarrytown, New York 10591-9001

Library of Congress Cataloging-in-Publication Data

Ayer, Eleanor H.
    Poland : a troubled past, a new start / Eleanor Ayer.
        p.   cm. — (Exploring cultures of the world)
    Includes bibliographical references.
    Summary: Discusses the history, geography, daily life, culture, and customs of this country of northern east-central Europe.
    ISBN 0-7614-0198-9 (library binding)
    1. Poland—Juvenile literature.   [1. Poland.]   I. Title. II Series.
DK4147.A97   1996
943.8—dc20   95-25702

Printed and bound in the U.S.A.

Book design by Carol Matsuyama
Photo research by Sandy Jones

Front cover: A young couple in national costume
Back cover: A shepherd with his flock in Zawoja

Photo Credits

Front cover: courtesy of TRAVELPIX/FPG International; back cover: courtesy of Joe Vesti/Vesti Assoc., Inc.; title page: courtesy of Jarek Iwansi/Sovfoto/Eastfoto; page 6: Archive Photos; pages 9, 26: David Woodfall/Natural History Photographic Agency, Sussex, England; page 11: Giraudon/Art Resource, NY; pages 13, 54, 55 *(top)*: The Bettmann Archive; pages 15, 55 *(bottom)*: Reuters/Bettmann Newsphotos; page 16: Interfoto MTI, Hungary/Sovfoto/Eastfoto; pages 18, 32: Carl Purcell/WORDS & PICTURES; pages 23, 38, 40: Witold Skrypczak/Tom Stack & Associates; page 25: Kelly Culpepper/Transparencies, Inc.; page 28: TRAVELPIX/FPG International; page 30: Ulrike Welsch; page 31: Greg Gilman/FPG International; page 35: David Constantine/Panos Pictures, London; page 37: Peter Hirth/Sovfoto/Eastfoto; page 42: Jeremy Hartley/Panos Pictures, London; page 44: Jarek Iwansi/Sovfoto/Eastfoto; page 45: FPG International; page 46: Andrea Pistolesi/The Image Bank; page 47: Russ Adams/Russ Adams Productions; page 48: Henryk T. Kaiser/Transparencies, Inc.; page 51: Stefan Kraszewski/Sovfoto/Eastfoto; page 52: Hackett/Archive Photos; page 57: Mirek Szepietowski/Sovfoto/Eastfoto

Contents

Polish and American military hero Tadeusz Kościuszko

1

People of the Plain

In front of the White House, where the president lives in Washington D.C., stands a statue of a hero, the Polish army officer Tadeusz Kościuszko (taw-DEH-ohsh kaws-ee-US-ko). The statue was built to honor the man who was such a great help to the American colonists during the Revolutionary War.

Kościuszko was born in 1746 in the Polish Lithuanian Commonwealth. His parents sent him to Warsaw, the Polish capital, to study at a military school. After he finished school, Kościuszko was hired as a private teacher for two daughters of a Polish nobleman. He fell in love with one, and they made a grand plan to run away and get married. But the plan failed. Rather than face the girl's angry father, Kościuszko decided to flee.

In 1776 he sailed for America. Here he joined the colonists who were fighting for freedom from the British in the Revolutionary War. For a time Kościuszko served as an aide to General Horatio Gates. At the end of the war the grateful colonists made him a citizen of the newly formed United States of America. Congress gave him land and money for his services.

But Kościuszko was anxious to get back to Poland. The Russians *were trying to invade his country, and the Polish army needed his help. Kościuszko rose quickly to the rank of major general. In 1794 the Polish people proclaimed him national commander and commander in chief of all military forces. That year he led a revolt against the invaders. The Russian army had many more troops and weapons than Kościuszko's forces. Still, the Polish army fought bravely with the help of farmers and peasants, armed only with the scythes used to cut grain in their fields.*

On the day his troops won the battle at Raclawice, Kościuszko became a hero. But disaster lay just around the corner. Soon after, he was wounded in battle and taken as a prisoner to Russia. Without their leader the Polish peasants could not keep up their fight. Within a year Poland had been divided among Russia, Austria, and Prussia, and the country existed no more.

In 1796 Kościuszko was freed from prison and returned home. The Russians offered him his sword and a large piece of land on which he could build an estate. But he refused both. "I have no more need of a sword," he told them, "as I have no longer a country."

To the Polish people Kościuszko remained a hero. When he died in 1817, his body was taken to Wawel Cathedral in the city of Kraków, to be buried with kings. Outside Kraków the people piled a huge mound of soil collected from battlefields all across Poland.

The Lay of the Land

One reason that Poland has had trouble defending itself is its geography. It has few natural barriers. The country is a wide, flat lowland in northern east-central Europe. From the huge plain that stretches across it comes the nation's Polish name: Polanie, "people of the plain."

On the west lies Germany, whose troops overran Poland in 1939 and started World War II. Many times in its history Poland

A farmstead in Wigierski National Park. Poland, mostly a lowland plain, also has forests of pine and spruce trees.

has fought armies invading from the east, especially from Russia. Today the eastern boundary is shared by three countries: Ukraine, Belarus (formerly part of the Soviet Union), and Lithuania. A small piece of Russia touches Poland on the north, but along most of its northern boundary lies the Baltic Sea.

In the south two narrow mountain ranges form Poland's only natural barrier. The Sudeten Mountains in the southwest separate the country from the Czech Republic. In the southeast the Carpathians form the border with Slovakia. The tallest peaks in Poland—the High Tatras, which reach 8,200 feet

(2,500 meters)—are in the Carpathian Mountains. The country's longest and most important river is the Vistula. It begins in the Carpathian Mountains and flows north to the Baltic Sea.

Poland is slightly smaller than the state of New Mexico, but it has twenty-five times as many people. The entire population of New Mexico could live in Poland's capital city of Warsaw—with room to spare! Warsaw, with more than 1.6 million people, lies in east-central Poland on both banks of the Vistula River. Lodz (looj), the second largest city, is in the very center of the country.

Forests filled with spruce and pine trees cover nearly a quarter of Poland. They thrive in its damp, moderate climate. The country is home to interesting animals, such as wildcats, lynx, chamois (antelope), and bears. European bison were once as common in Poland as American bison were on the Great Plains. But like their American cousins, the European bison are now more rare.

Poland's Early History

Historians know very little about Poland before the 900s. Early in the tenth century, tribes of Slavic people moved in from the south. One tribe was called the Polanie. They settled near today's city of Poznan. The Polanie's chief, Piast, united the many scattered tribes and gave the country its name.

The first leader to rule all of Poland was Mieszko I. During his time Christianity came to Poland. Mieszko himself became a Christian in 966, the year historians call the official birth of Poland. Mieszko expanded the country. By the time he died in 992, Poland was nearly as large as it is today.

Mieszko's son, Boleslaw I, became one of Poland's most powerful rulers. He extended the country's borders and built

A painting of Warsaw, the country's capital, in 1770, when Poland was still whole and strong.

the capital near Poznan. Just before Boleslaw died in 1025, the pope crowned him as Poland's first king.

Many years of war followed. At last, in the late 1400s, Poland entered a golden age, and for the next two centuries Poland was one of the most powerful countries in Europe. New towns sprang up and the older ones grew. Businesses

11

thrived and schools were built. In 1364 a university was founded in Kraków, one of the oldest in central Europe. The country's eastern border reached all the way to the Black Sea in what is now Russia. The capital was moved to Warsaw in 1596 to be closer to the center of the country.

Then war came again. During the 1600s and 1700s, the Poles fought many enemies. One of their brightest leaders was King John Sobieski, who saved Vienna and western Europe from the Ottoman Turks. But neither he nor Poland's other heroes were able to save their country.

In 1772 Russia, Austria, and Prussia captured a third of Poland to divide among themselves. This was the first partition, or division. Twenty-one years later, Russia and Prussia struck again, conquering another third of the country. Desperate to save what little land remained, the Polish nation made a last stand in 1794, led by the Polish military hero Tadeusz Kościuszko. But the struggle was in vain. In 1795 the third and last partition wiped Poland from world maps for the next 123 years.

The Country in Modern Times

Twice in the nineteenth century, Poles tried to free themselves from harsh Russian, German, and Austrian rule. But not until the defeat of Russia and Germany at the end of World War I, in 1918, was Poland reborn. The rebirth got off to a very shaky start, though. Nearly one million Poles had been killed in the war. The land was in ruins, and people were out of money. Ignacy Paderewski, one of Poland's greatest pianists and composers, became prime minister. The head of the country was Józef Piłsudski, who later took over as dictator.

In nearby Germany, Adolf Hitler had formed the Nazi

This cartoon, drawn in 1772, shows a map of Poland under dispute during the first partition. At the left, pointing: *Catherine II of Russia;* at the right: *Frederick of Prussia. Trying to hold his country together is Stanislav* (center), *the last king of independent Poland.*

Party and was making plans to conquer all of Europe. At dawn on September 1, 1939, Germany invaded Poland from the west, starting World War II. At the same time, armies from the Soviet Union invaded from the east. The combined attack was too much, and the Poles were forced to surrender. Poland was then divided between Germany and Soviet Russia as a result of an agreement between Hitler and Joseph Stalin, the leader of the Soviet Union.

The Nazis were extremely cruel to the Poles. By the millions they hauled them into concentration camps and made them work as slaves until they died of illness or starvation. More than six million Poles perished during World War II. Half of them were Jews, and the others were Christians. Hitler hated both the Jews and the Poles.

POLISH GOVERNMENT

The Republic of Poland, Rzeczpospolita Polska, is a parliamentary republic. Its representatives in Parliament are elected by the people. The most powerful branch of government is the Sejm, one of the two houses of Parliament. Its 460 members are elected for four years. The other house, the Senat (Senate), has 100 members. Poland is headed by a president, who serves a five-year term. The president nominates a prime minister, who is the head of government.

The highest law is the constitution, written in 1952 during Communist rule. Beginning in 1989, many changes have been made to the constitution.

Poland has so many political parties that it is difficult for any one of them to win a majority of votes in an election.

When the war ended in 1945, Germany had lost and Soviet armies had taken over all of Poland. This meant the country was now ruled by a Communist government. Life under communism was strict and harsh. Many people lived in fear of being reported to the police or arrested and killed for no reason.

The Communist government tried to control most of the land and businesses. But the peasants, with the help of the Catholic Church, fought to hold on to most of their land.

The Poles held strikes and protests and staged revolts to free themselves from communism. Most of these actions

Solidarity workers gather for a rally at the Solidarity Worker's Monument in Gdańsk.

15

Former Polish president Lech Wałesa in 1995, before Aleksander Kwasniewski took his place.

brought small victories, but from the 1950s through the 1970s the Communists stayed strong and the Poles remained poor.

In 1980 shipbuilders in the city of Gdańsk went on strike. They refused to work until conditions in their country improved. Workers from all parts of Poland joined the strike. They formed a group called Solidarity, which means unity. Its leader was Lech Wałesa. During the next ten years Solidarity held many strikes and peaceful protests.

At last in 1989 the Communists agreed to let the people hold elections. The next year candidates from the Solidarity Party won many seats in the parliament. Wałesa was elected president, and communism came to an end in Poland. For five years he ruled the country. But as his power increased, his popularity decreased. Some people felt Wałesa was becoming too much like a dictator. Others were upset because his promises of a better life for Poles were not happening smoothly or quickly enough.

Voters showed their unhappiness in late 1995. Lech Wałesa was not reelected president. In his place they chose Aleksander Kwasniewski (kvash-NYEF-skee), a former Communist. Kwasniewski promised "to cope with the problems of unemployment, of the poor and with the situation of Polish women." But many fear that his election may mean a return to Communist ways. Like many former Communist countries, Poland is finding that the change to a free government can be long and very difficult.

A Polish boy feeds pigeons in Kraków, the only Polish city not heavily damaged in World War II.

2

THE PEOPLE

Meet the Poles

If your name is Tomasz (Thomas) and your birthday is May 30, you probably won't celebrate it until September 22. Why? Because this is the first day after your birth date that "Tomasz" appears on the Polish name calendar. Every day on this special calendar has the name of a saint or king from long ago. Often when Polish children are born they are given the name of a saint or a king along with their own name. It is the Polish custom to celebrate your birthday on the day that your saint or king's name first appears on the calendar. If it appears more than once, as it does for Tomasz, you celebrate on the first name day after your own day of birth.

Tomasz (which means "twin") is a common name in Poland, just as Thomas is in the United States. Many other well-known English names are common in Poland. Stefania and Stefa are Polish ways of saying Stephanie; Elka or Elzbieta is Polish for Elizabeth, as are Krysztof and Piotr for Christopher and Peter.

Not all Polish names have English equivalents. The girl's name Wladyslawa (vlah-dis-SLAW-vah) means "petite" or "feminine." Teodozji (the-o-DOZ-yee) stands for "gift of God." Miroslawy (MEE-ro-slaw-vee) means "peace" or "glory." Often you can tell a Polish last name because it ends in *ski*. Other common Polish name endings are *icki* or *wicz*.

A Hardworking People

Poland has nearly 39 million people. Two-thirds of them live in cities. Upper Silesia, near the Czech Republic, is home to one out of every ten Poles. Many of them live near the city of Katowice.

Like many countries of Europe, Poland is quite crowded. On average, 318 people live on each square mile (2.6 square kilometers) of land. Compare that to the state of New Mexico, which is about the same size as Poland but has only 13 people per square mile!

Most of Poland's people are Slavic. They often have blond or light brown hair and light-colored eyes. Their roots go back many centuries to the time of the Polanie and other Slavic tribes. Other ethnic groups live in Poland today, but their numbers are small.

"A guest in the house is God in the house" is an old Polish saying. Poles are friendly, warm, and generous to visitors. They tend to be fun loving and enjoy a good joke.

Poles are often conservative: They don't take risks or chances. In making decisions, they look to religion or to the teachings of their ancestors. Polish people are also very hard workers. Generations of harsh living have taught them that there are no easy routes through life.

Speaking Polish

Around the country there are many regional accents or slightly different ways of speaking. The language spoken in western

SAY IT IN POLISH

Yes	*Tak* (tawk)
No	*Nie* (nyeh)
Please	*Proszę* (PRO-sheh)
Thank you	*Dziękuję* (DINK-wee-um)
How are you?	*Co słychać* (ZSO zvee-hach)
Good-bye	*Do widzenia* (doh veet-ZEN-yuh)

Numbers

1 *jeden* (YEH-den)
2 *dwa* (d-VAH)
3 *trzy* (tzrih—make a sound like a bird chirping!)
4 *cztery* (zt-TARE-ee)
5 *pięć* (pee-YENCH)
6 *sześć* (schescht)
7 *siedem* (SHED-em)
8 *osiem* (AWSH-em)
9 *dziewięć* (JEV-yinch)
10 *dziesięć* (JESH-inch)

POLISH PROVERB

In the United States, it's the groundhog that predicts how much longer winter will last, depending on whether it sees its shadow on February 2. In Poland, that prediction is made on Christmas Eve:

Na Adama pięknie,
zima rychło pęknie.

If it's bright on St. Adam's Day (December 24),
winter will soon be over.

Poland, around Poznan, is what Americans think of as Polish.

There are thirty-two letters in the Polish alphabet, but not all are the same as in English. There is no letter *q*. *V* and *x* appear only in foreign words that have made their way into Polish. *Z* is one of the most common letters in the Polish language. There are three letters *z*. Two of them have diacritical, or "sound," marks that change the way these letters sound. Diacritical marks on Polish letters are very important because they give the letters a completely new pronunciation. For example, plain *l* is pronounced like the English *l*. But *ł* (*l* with a line through it) has the sound of *w* in *wine*. Polish can be difficult to learn for people who do not know other Slavic languages, such as Czech and Slovak. The grammar is complicated, and words are pronounced very differently from those in English and most Western European languages. Ninety-nine percent of Poles speak Polish. It is the official language of the country. But many younger people, especially those who live around cities, also speak English or German.

Worshiping God

For many centuries Poles have been strong Roman Catholics. But when the Communists were in power, they tried to wipe out religion. People were discouraged from going to church, and some priests were sent to prison. But even though religion was outlawed in Poland, people continued to pray in private. In 1956 the citizens revolted. They demanded the right to go to church. At last the Communist government gave in. Leaders realized that banning religion had only made the Poles' faith stronger.

Today 95 percent of Poles are practicing Roman Catholics. Religion is a very big part of Polish life. Pictures of Christ and

Inside Bernardine Church in the Małopolska region. This is one of the many ornate Catholic churches whose steeples rise above Polish villages and towns.

the Virgin Mary hang in many homes. On Sundays people dress in their best clothes and go to mass at one of the thousands of Catholic churches.

Before World War II there were three million Jews in Poland. For centuries, the Poles had allowed Jews into their country when some other European nations had not. Very few Polish Jews survived the Nazi concentration camps. Those who did found themselves unwelcome when they returned home. This time it was not the Nazis who forced them out. It was the Polish people under the influence of the Communist regime. In 1968, when anti-Semitism—a hatred of Jews— reached a new peak, thousands of Polish Jews fled in fear. Fewer than 5,000 Jews make their home in Poland today.

Out of Step in the Modern World

One-third of all Poles work at industrial jobs. Factories make steel, glass, chemicals, cloth, and vehicles such as cars, trains, and ships. The country has a good supply of natural resources, such as coal, lead, copper, and nickel, that are used in manufacturing. Poland also has some of the world's largest deposits of sulfur and zinc.

Yet stepping into a Polish factory is like stepping back in time fifty years. Only a few of the factories are modern. In most the machinery is old and broken. In place of high-speed computers and lasers are laborers who work with worn-out tools. The buildings are dingy and dirty. Chimneys blow black smoke that pollutes the air and the countryside. During their forty years of rule, the Communists did little to improve Poland's factories. Since the fall of communism, the people have been struggling to rebuild their businesses and industries.

Agriculture is also a major part of the economy. About

*Pollution pours from a power plant near Katowice, a city in the center of
Poland's industrial region.*

A farmer loads a hay wagon the old-fashioned way on his farm in eastern Poland.

half the land is good for raising crops. The most important one is rye, but farmers also grow potatoes, wheat, sugar beets, barley, and oats. About a third of the Polish people are farmers. But their ways of farming are as outdated as the machinery in Polish factories. Many farmers still use horses instead of tractors, and they walk behind plows to till their fields.

The old ways make it hard for Polish farmers to raise enough to feed their people. Poland must still import many of the food products it needs. In order to produce high-quality products that people and businesses want to buy, Poland needs to modernize its farms and factories. Since 1989, when the Communists left the country, Poland's economy has been growing at a fast pace. American businesses are investing in Poland, which is helping the economy. Change will take a great deal of time and money, but it is on the way.

A Polish street vendor in colorful native costume displays his wares for tourists on a street in Kraków.

3

FAMILY LIFE, FESTIVALS, AND FOOD

Poles at Home

When former President Wałesa said, "My family is the foundation of my life," he was speaking for millions of Polish people. The family—along with the Catholic Church—is the center of Polish society. Traditions and customs mean a lot to the Poles.

Poles have a fierce love for all things Polish. They love their country even if they don't always love its government. Right now Poland is very poor. Many people have a hard time earning enough money to support a family. Many are out of work, too, and housing is hard to find.

In the City and in the Country

Because Poland is densely populated, city people often live in apartments. There is little room for gardens, so the people spend a lot of time in the parks. Many city people own cars. Most popular is the small Fiat. It doesn't use much gas, which is very expensive in Poland.

The nation has no superhighway system. Only short sections of freeways have been built. People still walk or ride

Farm vehicles often slow the pace of traffic on Polish streets and highways.

bicycles in the middle of the roads and expect drivers to go around them. In the countryside, tractors, wagons, and animals share the roads with cars.

Many rural people live in the same farmhouse where their great-grandparents grew up. Life on the farm means long hours of hard work. And even so, many farmers can barely scratch out a living. This is why many young people are anxious to leave the farms and move to the cities.

But for the Górale, farming may always be the way of life. These 150,000 people live high in the Tatra Mountains. On the beautiful green pastures of the Podhale, they raise sheep, goats, and dairy cattle. The Górale do not use modern farm equipment, and most live as their ancestors did hundreds of years ago. Women and children plant and care for the crops. Men tend the animals and work with machinery.

Three generations of a family sometimes live in the same

A Górale woman does farm chores by hand, much as her ancestors did.

house. Often they share just one or two rooms so they can rent the others to travelers. The Górale speak their own dialect. The men often dress in white jackets or shirts and tight white pants.

A Typical Polish Week

When it's shortly after midnight in New York, Polish children are probably having breakfast. School starts at eight o'clock. Younger children finish at about one in the afternoon. Older students go until two-thirty or later. Like many countries of Europe, Poland is on a twenty-four-hour clock, so one o'clock in the afternoon is 1300 hours. On the Polish calendar Monday (*Poniedziałek*) is the first day of the week.

Many Polish men work in coal mines. They start work

Warsaw children are on their way to begin another school day.

about six in the morning. Because mining is hard and dangerous work, miners get at least twenty-five days of vacation each year. Most Poles believe mothers should stay home with their children. However, today many women have to work outside the home because their families are poor.

Sunday is a day of rest. Few businesses are open, and most people go to church and then return home for a big meal. In the afternoon they visit with neighbors, play with friends, or browse at sidewalk booths where people sell food and bargain items.

Holy Days

This strong Catholic country has many religious holidays. Epiphany (*Dzień Trzech Króli*) is on January 6. Priests bless pieces of chalk with which people write K + M + B in front of their doors. The letters stand for the Polish names of the three wise men who supposedly came to visit the baby Jesus on this day.

Easter (*Wielkanoc*), and the holy days leading up to it in March and April, is nearly as important as Christmas. Since Catholics cannot work on Easter, cooking is done on Saturday. A priest blesses the food. Families paint boiled eggs and decorate them. Some take the eggs to church to be blessed, then cut them into slices to share with friends. Children play a game to see whose egg will last longest without breaking when tapped against other eggs.

Instead of the Easter bunny, Polish children celebrate with the Paschal Lamb, a symbol for Christ. Catholics decorate pastries and candies in the shape of lambs. The day after Easter is called Wet Monday. Boys run after girls, trying to douse them with cold water. Young men chase older girls to

33

RECIPE FOR ROYAL MAZUREK

The traditional Easter treat of Poland is a shortbread cake with a glaze sauce. The royal mazurek uses a chocolate glaze over the cake, but you can also make it with a coffee or caramel glaze. Don't forget to ask an adult for help with this, especially in separating the egg yolks.

Preheat oven to 325 degrees. Grease and flour a 9 x 12-inch pan. Gather the following ingredients:

1 cup flour
1/2 tablespoon baking powder
1/2 cup confectioners' sugar

1/2 teaspoon salt
1 cup almonds, chopped very fine

Mix these ingredients together and set aside. You'll be adding them to the ones below.

1 egg, beaten slightly,
and 1 more egg yolk

1/2 cup sour cream
1 stick soft butter or margarine

Cream together these ingredients. Add the dry mixture to them just a little bit at a time. The dough is stiff, so be sure you mix well each time you add.

Spread the mixture into the baking pan and bake on middle rack in oven for 30 minutes. The cake should be a nice light brown on top. While cake is cooling, make the glaze:

3 cups confectioners' sugar
6 tablespoons powdered cocoa

1/4 cup melted butter or margarine
1/4 cup whipping cream

Mix sugar and cocoa. Add cream and butter slowly, stirring until smooth. When cake is cool, spread glaze over the top. Decorate with pieces of candy, dried fruit, or nuts.

spray them with perfume. The next day it's the girl's turn to chase the boys! This custom is called *Smigus-Dyngus* (water dousing). It used to be done in the hope of bringing rain to newly planted fields.

Poles have many holidays honoring saints and ten special

A procession in Poznan on the Feast of Corpus Christi. Many of Poland's holidays are tied to the Catholic Church.

religious holidays called High Days. But the most celebrated is Christmas (*Boże Narodzenie*). All day on Christmas Eve (*Wigilia*), people fast—they eat nothing. When the first star shines that evening, family members break holy bread and wish one another a good year ahead. A twelve-course feast follows, with an extra place set at the table for an unexpected guest. Later the children go to the *choinka*, or Christmas tree, for their gifts. In some homes *Święty Mikołaj* (Santa Claus) passes out the presents. Next, everyone goes to Christmas Eve Mass at church. Christmas Day is spent with the family, feasting and going to church.

LEGEND OF THE CHRISTMAS SPIDERS

A *szopka* is a portable puppet theater in which Polish children put on plays. At Christmas children carry their *szopka* from house to house performing plays. You can make a *szopka* from a cardboard box about fifteen inches tall and twice as wide. You may want to perform the popular Legend of the Christmas Spiders.

It is said that in Poland animals can talk on Christmas Eve. On that night a boy was walking by a poor family's house and heard soft crying. Outside the door a group of spiders were huddled. They were sad because the family had a beautiful Christmas tree but were too poor to decorate it. If the spiders could open the door, they could help the family. Quickly the boy pushed open the door. The spiders scurried across the floor and up the tree, spinning a series of amazing webs that covered its branches.

The spiders did not know it was the Christ Child who had opened the door. Knowing that a mess of cobwebs on her tree would upset the mother greatly, the Christ Child blessed the tree and immediately the sticky gray webs turned to shimmering silver and gold. This is why people today decorate their Christmas trees with strands of shining tinsel!

A Time for Parades and Parties

Polish farmers have parades at fall harvesttime to thank God for good crops. The person leading the parade carries a cross. Girls make harvest wreaths out of corn and decorate them with figures of roosters or pretty girls. They dance down the road carrying the wreaths to farmers' homes. The next spring, the farmers plant the seeds from the wreaths. But before they do, it's time for the drowning of the Marzanna. This ugly old scarecrow is the symbol of winter. For hundreds of years the drowning of the Marzanna has been celebrated with parades and parties that mark the official end of winter.

Weddings are a time for big celebrations in Polish families. Guests dress in traditional clothing—white blouses or shirts with long puffed sleeves, topped by a vest or jacket with a beautiful embroidered design. Women's skirts may have colorful ribbons hanging from them. The ceremony in the church is followed by a huge wedding feast, with dancing that often lasts all night or even several days!

At breakfast the next day the bride and groom eat the wedding pastry: two rectangular cakes that were baked in the oven together. Then it's time for the "capping." Guests try to place a special cap on the bride's head to show that she is ready to leave her birth family and go with her husband. Since she is sad to be leaving her family, the bride pretends to run away to avoid the capping.

Special Foods

Eating at a Polish wedding feast is like dining in a castle. There are roasted geese and ducks, fancy pickles, Polish rye bread,

In a show of faith, Catholics join a yearly pilgrimage to Czestocowa.

A Polish family from Wrocław relaxes after obiad, *the midday meal.*

and cheeses and fruits of all sorts. The wedding cake is shaped like a ring. Some families also bake small, animal-shaped cakes for guests to throw at the bride and groom when the ceremony is over. Wine, beer, and vodka—the national drink— are usually served.

The Christmas Eve feast is nearly as special. Fish is served because Catholics may eat no meat on Christmas Eve. There are vegetables such as cabbage and mushrooms and usually a noodle dish.

Special Polish dinners often begin with soup (*zupa*). The country is famous for *barszcz* (borscht), a soup made from beets. Poles eat fish often, because it is cheaper and more available than meat. Pike, carp, salmon, flounder, and herring are in good supply. The most popular meats are sausage, pork, and beef. *Kiełbasa*, the Polish word for sausage, refers to a kind of uncooked, smoked sausage made in Poland and now eaten worldwide.

Farmers raise beets, barley, rye, and lots of potatoes, so noodles and breads are favorite foods. Golabki—cabbage roll—is a popular dish made of chopped meat and rice wrapped in cabbage leaves. Another favorite is bigos, in which sauerkraut (sour cabbage) is stuffed with spicy meat and vegetables, often mushrooms. For dessert Poles like such things as prune compote (prunes cooked in syrup) or a piece of poppy-seed cake.

Most Polish families eat four meals a day. Breakfast (*śniadanie*) may be sausage, cheese, and bread with butter and jam. The second breakfast (*drugie śniadanie*) is usually a sandwich, eaten between eleven o'clock and noon. *Obiad*, the big meal of the day, is eaten between three and six, in the late afternoon. The last meal of the day, *kolacja*, may be nearly as large as *obiad*, or just a roll and a glass of tea.

Bar mleczny, or "milk bars," were once common sights in Poland. These plain, self-service restaurants offered good Polish food, vegetarian dishes, and dairy products. Many have now closed or been turned into fast-food shops that serve food like flaki, a dish made of tripe (a cow's stomach lining) cooked in bouillon with vegetables. If flaki doesn't sound good, you can order a pizza or hamburger here. And like many other countries, Poland is now serving Coke and other American soft drinks.

A chess tournament involves players and onlookers in a town square.

4

SCHOOL AND RECREATION

School, Games, and Paper Cutouts

In Poland young people are a major part of the population. The average age in the country is twenty-nine. This is because so many Poles were killed during World War II. The survivors had many children. The children of these baby boomers are now in school. Education is very important in Polish life. Ninety-eight percent of Polish adults and older children can read and write. Nearly one-fifth have studied beyond high school. All education in Poland, no matter what level, is free (although that may soon change).

Going to School

Students must attend school (*szkoła;* SHKO-wa) from ages seven to eighteen. Children three to six years old may go to kindergarten. About half of them do. After elementary school those who want to go to college may take an exam to enter a lyceum, or preparatory school. Those who do not may choose a trade or vocational high school. Here they learn skills such as woodworking, mechanics, or computer science.

The Polish school year begins on September 1 and ends in

middle or late June. There are vacations at Christmas and Easter as well as a two-week break in the winter.

One of the biggest problems Poland faces in becoming more modern is teaching its citizens English. When the country was Communist, students studied Russian. But to do business today, Poles need to know English, along with French and German. Polish schools are now hiring thousands of teachers of English and other foreign languages.

These boys live in a state boarding home because their families are unable to raise them. They are learning how to work with wood.

Just for Fun

At recess children play games (*gry*) such as Running Fox (*Idzie Lis;* EE-tzhee lees). This game is a cross between Drop the Handkerchief and Duck, Duck, Goose. Eight or so children form a circle facing the center, hands behind their backs. One is chosen to be the fox. The fox parades around the circle carrying a handkerchief and chanting this verse in Polish:

> *This poor old fox, he wanders the land,*
> *Has no foot, and has no hand.*
> *A sad and sorry sight is he,*
> *Let's tan his hide with sympathy!*

While saying the rhyme, the fox stuffs the handkerchief into the hands of one of the other children. The child on that person's right must run around the outside of the circle, trying to avoid being touched by the handkerchief until he or she gets back "home" again. If the handkerchief touches, that person becomes the fox.

Another game is *Baba Jaga i Anioły* (ba-ba yah-jah ee ah-NYO-wee), The Witch and the Angels. One person is the witch, and the others are the angels. Using sticks or stones, the witch marks out a "cell" for prisoners and the angels mark out a "home," on opposite sides of the playing field. Dancing around in their home, the angels sing:

> *One, two, three, the witch is looking at me.*
> *Four, five, six, she knows a lot of tricks.*
> *Seven, eight, nine, on us she'd like to dine.*
> *She'll throw us to the stars,*
> *So, quick, let's run afar!*

At this the angels run, and the witch tries to catch them. An angel who is caught must go to the witch's cell. Other angels may rescue the captured ones by touching them. Angels may go "home" to rest in safety. When the witch captures all

Polish girls share a laugh. Poles are often thought to be serious, hardworking people, but they enjoy many kinds of entertainment.

the angels, he or she wins. But if, after some time, few or no angels have been caught, the game is over and the witch loses.

In Their Spare Time

Most Poles are hardworking people who have neither the time nor the money to spend on leisure activities. Still, when they have the chance, they like to enjoy themselves. A popular pastime for hundreds of years has been creating craftwork. In the small towns, local craftspeople weave rugs, tablecloths, and other beautiful tapestries. They make pottery, paint on glass and wood, do fancy wood carving, and embroider pretty flowers or other designs on cloth. Poles are famous for their handmade wooden spoons and boxes, which they decorate with colorful designs. They also crochet fine patterns in lace.

In the mid-1800s, Polish peasants began making *wycinanki* (vih-chee-NAN-kee), or paper cutouts. Using a glazed colored paper, they cut fancy flowers, roosters, hearts, and other stencil designs. Each spring they whitewashed their walls and put up new cutouts, hanging the old ones in their sheds or

44

barns. In the days before scissors, the women and girls used knives to make the cutouts. Travelers to Poland can buy *wycinanki* and other folk art in special *Cepelia* shops. Unfortunately many younger Poles do not care to learn the old crafts, and so these decorative arts may soon be forgotten.

When Poles go traveling, they like to visit the country's hundred or more castles. Most famous is Wawel Castle, high on a hill in Kraków. This magical place is one of the most visited spots in Poland. For more than five hundred years, Poland's kings ruled from Wawel's throne. On display are old weapons and even the jagged sword once used at the coronations of new kings in the castle's grand cathedral. Many of Poland's heroes are buried here. Among them are Tadeusz Kościuszko and Józef Piłsudski. According to legend, the castle

A peasant in native dress sits in his home in Zalipe. The village is noted for decorating its houses with colorful folk art and floral designs.

Wawel Castle, from which Polish kings ruled for more than five hundred years

even has a dragon named Smok Wawelski. If you visit the castle today, you will come upon this dragon, cast in bronze. It lives in a cave near the Thieves' Tower and spits fire! In addition to its castles Poland has a number of gorgeous palaces built by powerful royal families. Most are in the Warsaw area and are open to the public as museums.

Like people around the world, Poles watch television in their spare time. The country has two channels. One offers general-interest programs. The other has more educational and cultural shows. Satellite dishes are very popular, for they make it possible to watch programs from the United States and the Western European countries. Polskie Radio is the major radio network. You can hear headline news in English, but nearly all other programs are in Polish.

Soccer, Horseback Riding, and Winter Sports

Soccer is the favorite national sport, but it is not as big in Poland as in many other parts of Europe. The country has three leagues whose games attract many fans. The game is also the most popular team sport among children. They play at school or through private clubs. But Poland is not a wealthy country, and often neither the schools nor the children's families can afford to buy sports equipment.

Horseback riding has always been popular in Poland. Some people ride for pleasure. Others use their horses for hunting boar, deer, fox, and bison. November is the time for the Hubertus Run in many towns. Hubert is the patron saint of hunters. His day of honor is marked by a special fox hunt, in which riders chase a fox, trying to run it down.

Volleyball, basketball, swimming, field hockey, and ice hockey are other popular sports. Since the success of Wojtek Fibak, two-time Polish world champion in the seventies, there is now more interest in tennis. Poles also enjoy marathon running and motorcycle racing.

Wojtek Fibak, Polish tennis champion, playing in a tournament in New Hampshire, 1980.

Poland's lakes offer fine canoeing, swimming, and sailing. The High Tatras, in the Carpathian Mountains, are great places to hike, camp, and climb during the summer or ski in the winter. Zakopane is the largest and most popular ski area. Several international skiing events have been held there.

At a folk festival in Kraków, Poles celebrate their rich traditions.

5

THE ARTS

Polonaises and Poets

Asilhouette is a drawing or cutout in a solid color showing only the outline of a figure. In his book *Easter*, the Polish artist Jan Pieńkowski uses black silhouettes to illustrate the story of this Christian holiday. Around the silhouettes are bright, colorful background drawings, some edged in gilt.

Pieńkowski was born in Warsaw in 1936. After World War II he moved to England, where his love of drawing led him to become a designer. He has now illustrated more than thirty books. Two of them have won the top prize in England—the Kate Greenaway Medal—for children's book illustration. His book *Christmas* received the blessing of Pope John Paul II. You may have read Pieńkowski's *Haunted House* or *Robot* pop-up books.

Painting Their Hopes and Dreams

Early artists painted religious figures or scenes from the Bible. Their work often decorated churches. Later, kings and royal families were the subjects of paintings. In the mid-1800s artists turned to Polish history for their ideas, often making the scenes glamorous and heroic. Jan Matejko, one of Poland's best artists, painted during the time of the partitions. His paintings made people feel patriotic and proud rather than defeated and discouraged. In his painting *Copernicus in the Tower of Frombork*, Matejko brings to life the famous Polish astronomer as he sits in his tower watching the moon and stars.

In the late 1800s and early 1900s, when Poland was still divided, people lived in fear and hatred of the government. Jacek Malczewski's paintings show this feeling. In *Sunday in a Mine*, a group of Polish citizens have been shipped to Siberia— the cold, barren part of northern Russia—for speaking out against the government. Today, Polish artists often paint imaginative pictures rather than real life. The best painter of modern times may be Zdzisław Beksiński, born in 1929. Beksiński paints haunting, mysterious scenes out of dreams— quite different from Polish artists of earlier times. During the 1960s, poster art became very popular in Poland. Several painters now produce these beautiful, colorful posters. The Muzeum Plakatu (*plakat* means "poster") in Warsaw has collections of this art.

Lofty Churches and Castles

Until the mid-1200s, Poles created buildings in a style of architecture called Romanesque. These structures were made of stone and had a cold, stern look. In the thirteenth and fourteenth centuries, Gothic came into style. Buildings had high pointed arches with ribbed ceilings and roofs. Gothic architects built large churches and castles, many of which still stand today.

During the Renaissance period in the 1500s, builders used a more delicate, "pretty" style of architecture. Renaissance structures were not huge and awesome like Gothic buildings.

This intricate Gothic arch—called the Golden Gate—was built in a Warsaw church in 1417.

Instead they had fancy decorations and round, pleasing archways. In the 1600s the Renaissance style gave way to the Baroque, which used lavish, lacy decorations. You can see Baroque architecture today inside many old Polish churches and palaces.

By the 1800s architects were looking backward in time to get new ideas. They called their new designs *neo*-Gothic or *neo*-Renaissance (*neo* means a new twist on an old idea).

In the late 1940s and 1950s the Soviets brought in their own sense of design. Communist buildings were huge, boring

51

blocks of concrete. Since 1990 architects have started to design buildings in a more pleasing, interesting style.

Polkas and Polonaises

Along with talented artists and architects, Poland has given the world some great musicians. The country has two unique dances. One is the polonaise, an old Polish court dance. The composer who wrote the finest polonaises was Frédéric Chopin, who lived in the early 1800s. Chopin's music showed a deep love for his country. Upset because his homeland had been overtaken by Russia, he refused to play his twelve triumphant polonaises for Russian audiences.

The other truly Polish dance is the mazurka, in which dancers twirl, stamp their feet, and click their heels. Originally the mazurka was a folk dance. But Chopin made it the music of Poland by writing fifty-eight mazurkas for the piano.

The polka (meaning "Polish woman") is often thought of as a Polish dance. But it did not have its roots in Poland. It began in the 1830s as a folk dance in Bohemia, in

Polish composer Frédéric Chopin

what is now the Czech Republic. Soon it spread to other countries of Europe. Polka music is fun and lively, often played on an accordion.

At the Theater

Poles enjoy watching plays at the country's ninety-one theaters and twenty-four puppet theaters. Many Polish plays, especially those written during the Communist years, make fun of the government. In the 1960s the Polish director Jerzy Grotowski started the popular "laboratory theater." People in the audience were invited to take parts on stage, and the performers served as their helpers.

Movies are also a popular pastime. In fact one of the world's finest filmmakers comes from Poland. Roman Polanski, born in 1933, grew up in Kraków. In the early 1960s he became world famous with his film *Knife in the Water*. In the United States he wrote and directed *Rosemary's Baby*, *Chinatown*, and other well-known films.

Very few films shown in Poland are made there. Many are made in the United States and "dubbed," or translated, for Polish viewers. Sometimes the same dubbing voice is used for all the characters. This makes it hard to follow the movie, because you're not sure who is speaking.

Poland's Prize-Winning Authors

Like the artists, Polish poets and writers have helped pull their country together when enemies were tearing it apart. The poet Adam Mickiewicz, who wrote in the early 1800s, was arrested for writing poems that praised Poland. He was shipped to Russia, but this did not stop him from writing. About the same time two other poets, Juliusz Słowacki and Zygmunt Krasiński,

POLISH GREATS

Nicholas Copernicus (Mikolaj Kopernik) (1473–1543). This astronomer and mathematician was born in Toruń, in north-central Poland. In his day scientists thought the earth was the center of the universe and that the sun revolved around the earth. Copernicus disagreed. He believed that the earth turns on its axis and revolves around the sun like other planets. This idea is the basis of modern astronomy.

Joseph Conrad (Józef Teodor Konrad Korzeniowski) (1857–1924). This Polish-born author changed his name to Joseph Conrad after he became a British citizen. As a sailor he traveled to distant parts of the world, which he later used as settings for his books. *Lord Jim* is a novel of the sea. *Heart of Darkness* was set in Africa.

A hand-colored photograph of Marie Curie in her laboratory in 1915

Marie Curie (1867–1934). Born in Warsaw, Marya Skłodowska (her Polish name) went to Paris, France, to study. There she fell in love with a young physics teacher, Pierre Curie. They married and began working together. In 1898 they discovered the element radium. Five years later they won the Nobel Prize in physics—one of the highest science awards in the world. After Pierre died, Marie won a second Nobel Prize, in 1911, this one in chemistry. She was the first scientist to receive two Nobel Prizes.

were also driven from their homes for writing patriotic poetry.

In 1905 the Polish writer Henryk Sienkiewicz won the Nobel Prize in literature, one of the highest awards a writer can receive. His famous novel *Quo Vadis?* is the story of Rome in the days of the evil emperor Nero.

A more modern poet and writer, Czeslaw Milosz, won the Nobel Prize in 1980. His most famous book, *The Captive Mind,*

Arthur (Artur) **Rubenstein** (1887–1982). When he was three years old, Rubenstein could play pieces on the piano that he had heard only once before. His hands could reach even the widest chords. Rubenstein became a celebrated pianist, best known for playing the works of Chopin.

Polish pianist Arthur Rubenstein

Pope John Paul II (1920–   ). Karol Wojtyla, head of the Roman Catholic Church, was born in Wadowice, near the city of Kraków. When Pope John Paul I died in 1978, the fifty-eight-year-old Wojtyla became pope. He took the name John Paul II. He is the first pope ever chosen from Poland and the first non-Italian to head the Roman Catholic Church in 455 years.

Pope John Paul II at the Vatican in 1991

is a strong criticism of communism. A popular Polish author who lived in the United States was Jerzy Kosinski, known worldwide for his book, *The Painted Bird*, which he wrote in English.

"Poland drives out all its talented people," wrote the author James Michener in his book *Poland*. He was right. Over the years some of Poland's most creative writers, musicians,

KRENCIPAL AND KRENCIPALKA: A POLISH FAIRY TALE

Once a poor couple who lived on the plains of Poland set out to seek their fortune. Krencipal and Krencipalka had just begun their journey when they ran into a needle who begged:

"Take me with you all the way; I will help you night and day."

The couple agreed, and Krencipalka stitched the needle into her hat. On the way they met a lobster, a duck, a cock, a pig, an ox, and a horse, all of whom joined them.

By late afternoon they had reached a huge, dark wood. No one lived there because an evil goblin was said to haunt a house just inside the forest. But Krencipal and Krencipalka were not afraid. They went boldly into the house, and the needle made itself comfortable sticking up from a crack in a wooden bench. The lobster lodged in a bucket of water, while the pig ordered that a fire be built and some acorns roasted on it. The ox and horse went to the barn. The cock and duck curled up for naps.

When the evil goblin returned, Krencipal and Krencipalka explained that they were weary travelers. The goblin sat down to talk with them, but he landed squarely upon the needle! Jumping up in pain he ran to the water bucket to wash his wound. But when he reached in to scoop some water—CRACK—the lobster clamped down on his fingers. Three sharp bangs rang from the fireplace as the roasting acorns popped and hit him in the eye.

Terrified, the goblin ran from the house. Cries of "Quack, quack" from the duck and "Tuck, tuck" from the cock followed him. As he flew into the barn, the ox caught him on his horns and tossed him into the horse stall. The horse kicked him toward the Underworld, where he saw some people he knew.

"My house is haunted by humans," he stammered. "When I sat down on the bench, the cook was hiding beneath it and stuck me with a poker. I ran for the water bucket, but a mechanic with strange tools grabbed my hand. I pulled away but was shot at by someone in the fireplace. Then I heard voices calling, 'Smack, smack him well,' and 'Chuck, chuck him out.' In the barn someone with a pitchfork tossed me into a blacksmith's forge, where I was hit with a huge hammer. I will never go back to that house again." And so Krencipal and Krencipalka lived happily in the house with the needle, the lobster, the pig, the duck, the cock, the ox, and the horse!

artists, and scientists have fled from harsh governments to continue their work in other countries. Today, lack of money drives artists from home. They cannot survive in a country that is so poor. Still, most Poles' love for their country is fierce, and they are determined to make their land stronger and more stable in the years ahead.

Street musicians in the city of Gdańsk

Country Facts

Official name: Rzeczpospolita Polska (Republic of Poland)

Capital: Warsaw

Location: in east-central Europe, bordered on the north by Russia and the Baltic Sea; on the east by Ukraine, Belarus, and Lithuania; on the south by the Czech Republic and Slovakia; and on the west by Germany.

Area: 120,727 square miles (312,683 square kilometers). *Greatest distances:* east–west, 422 miles (680 kilometers); north–south, 403 miles (650 kilometers).

Elevation: *Highest:* Rysy Peak in the Carpathian Mountains, 8,200 feet (2,500 meters). *Lowest:* sea level along the Baltic coast.

Climate: moderate to cool. Temperatures are milder along the coast than inland; coolest temperatures are in the southern mountains.

Population: 38,400,000; 64 percent live in cities; 36 percent live in small towns or rural areas

Form of government: republic; headed by a president

Important products: *Natural Resources:* coal, sulfur, copper, natural gas, silver, lead, nickel, zinc. *Agriculture:* flax, rye, potatoes, wheat, sugar beets, barley, oats. *Industries:* steel, glass, chemicals, cloth, shipbuilding, machine building.

Basic unit of money: złoty; 1 złoty = 100 groszy

Language: Polish

Religion: 95 percent Roman Catholic; others are Russian Orthodox, Protestant, Muslim

Flag: two horizontal blocks: white on top, red on the bottom. The flag has no pictures or designs.

National Anthem: *Jeszcze Polska Nie Zginela* ("Poland Is Not Yet Lost")

Major holidays: New Year's Day; Epiphany, January 6; Good Friday, Friday before Easter; Easter; Wet Monday, Monday after Easter; Constitution Day, May 3; Corpus Christi, May or June; Assumption Day, August 15; All Saint's Day, November 1; Independence Day, November 11; Christmas

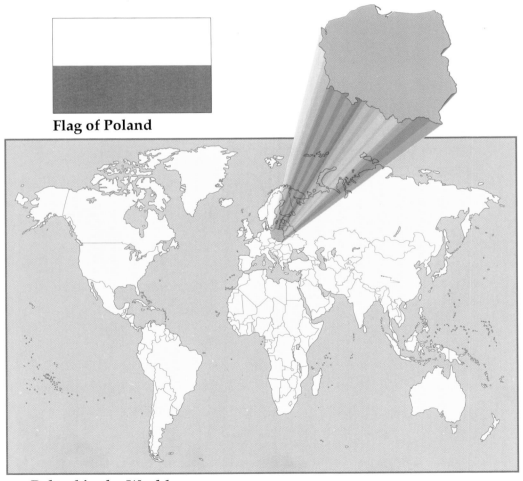

Flag of Poland

Poland in the World

Glossary

barszcz (borsch): Poland's famous soup made from beets, called in English "borscht"

communism: a type of government in which all property and goods are owned by the government and are shared equally by the people

concentration camps: labor camps built by the Nazis in Poland and other European countries during World War II. In these camps, millions of people were put to death.

diacritical marks (di-uh-KRIT-ih-kul): accents or other kinds of marks that show how a word is to be pronounced. The Polish language uses diacritical marks on several letters of the alphabet.

Górale (GOO-rawl): means "highlanders" and refers to the shepherds and farmers who live in the Podhale, in the High Tatra Mountains of southwest Poland

kiełbasa (kee-oo-BAW-suh): type of Polish sausage that is also popular in other parts of the world

mazurka (muh-ZURK-uh): lively Polish dance and the music that accompanies it. Frédéric Chopin made it the music of Poland by writing fifty-eight mazurkas for the piano.

partition: a separation or division. Poland suffered three partitions of its land by enemies.

polonaise (pawl-uh-NAZE): stately Polish dance and the music that accompanies it. Beautiful polonaises were written by the Polish composer Frédéric Chopin.

Solidarity (sawl-ih-DARE-ih-tee): union formed by Polish workers in 1980 to protest life under communism. Under the leadership of Lech Wałesa, Solidarity helped bring about the downfall of communism in Poland.

Soviet: having to do with a Communist government, particularly during the time of the former Soviet Union—the Union of Soviet Socialist Republics

For Further Reading

Remember: when using books about Poland that were published before 1990, some information may be incorrect because Poland is no longer controlled by the Communists.

Bradley, John. *Eastern Europe: The Road to Democracy.* New York: Gloucester Press, 1990.

Constable, George, ed. *Library of Nations: Eastern Europe.* Alexandria, VA: Time-Life Books, 1986.

Greene, Carol. *Enchantment of the World: Poland.* Chicago: Childrens Press, 1994.

Haviland, Virginia. *Favorite Fairy Tales Told in Poland.* Boston: Little, Brown, 1963.

Heale, Jay. *Poland,* Cultures of the World. New York: Marshall Cavendish, 1994.

Holland, Gini. *Poland Is My Home.* Milwaukee: Gareth Stevens, 1993.

Horn, Alfred, and Bozena Pietras. *Insight Guides: Poland.* Singapore: APA Publications, 1992.

Krzysztof, Dydyński. *Poland: A Travel Survival Kit.* Berkeley: Lonely Planet Publications, 1993.

Madison, Arnold. *Polish Greats.* New York: McKay, 1980.

Porazinska, Janina. *The Enchanted Book: A Tale from Krakow.* San Diego: Harcourt Brace Jovanovich, 1987.

Zamojska-Hutchins, Danuta. *Cooking the Polish Way.* Minneapolis: Lerner Publications, 1984.

Index

Page numbers for illustrations are in boldface

About the Author

Eleanor H. Ayer is the author of more than two dozen books for children and young adults, including *Germany* in the *Exploring* Cultures of the World series. Many of her books deal with social or historical issues, and she has also written several biographies.

Ms. Ayer holds a master's degree in literacy journalism from Syracuse University's Newhouse School. She lives with her husband and two sons in a town north of Denver, Colorado, where the Ayers operate a small book publishing company.